50 Early Finishers for 4th Grade

Lucky Jenny Publishing

The worksheets are © Elizabeth Chapin-Pinotti . (c) 2015 Lucky Jenny. Plymouth, California. www.luckyjenny.com.

The Clip Art is: by: www.whimsyclips.com, or www.teacherspayteachers.com/Store/Whimsy-Clips or www.etsy.com/shop/WhimsyClipArt

In This Packet

#1	Farmer Fred Math	#25	Puzzle Play
#2	Farmer Frannie Math	#26	Puzzle Play
#3	From the Barn Math	#27	Puzzle Play
#4	Searching for Patterns Math	#28	In Other Words…Synonym Practice
#5	The Number 84 Math	#29	In Other Words…Synonym Practice
#6	Farmer Fred's Multiplication Fluency	#30	In Other Words…Synonym Practice
#7	Farmer Fred Area and Perimeter	#31	In Other Words…Synonym Practice
#8	Farmer Fred A Way with Words	#32	Your Words…My Story…Creative Writing
#9	Create a Cover for Your Favorite Book	#33	Your Words…My Story…Creative Writing
#10	My Favorite Media in Four Panels	#34	Your Words…My Story…Creative Writing
#11	Alternative Endings	#35	Your Words…My Story…Creative Writing
#12	Rain for Farmer Fred Math	#36	Your Words…My Story…Creative Writing
#13	Finish Fractured Fairy Tale	#37	Sort it Out…Word Sort
#14	Finish Fractured Fairy Tale	#38	Sort it Out…Word Sort
#15	Finish Fractured Fairy Tale	#39	Sort it Out…Word Sort
#16	Finish Fractured Fairy Tale	#40	Sort it Out…Word Sort
#17	What's in the Bag	#41	Another Word For…Synonym Word Search
#18	Tell Me What You Think	#42	Another Word For…Synonym Word Search
#19	My Hero	#43	My Grocery List
#20	All in the Word Family	#44	My Dinner Menu
#21	All in the Word Family	#45	Trip to the Beach Vacation Plan
#22	Create your Own Country	#46	What if You Won the Lottery
#23	Puzzle Play	#47	What if You Were Principal for the Day
#24	Puzzle Play	#48	Create a Comic Strip
		#49	Polar Bears
		#50	Hippopotamus

Farmer Fred -- #1

Farmer Fred fretted over his fields of alfalfa. During a fair year, he planted 50 acres. During a frighteningly dry year he planted 44 acres. This year, lions and tigers and bears invaded his fields and took over 6 acres of what he'd already planted.

Fact: It was a _____ year.
Fact: Farmer Fred plants _____ acres during a _____ year.

Problem: How many acres of alfalfa will Farmer Fred have left to take to market?

Solve:

Explain...how did you get your answer: _____
_____
_____
_____

Write your own Farmer Fred Story Problem and solve.
_____
_____
_____
_____
_____
_____

Farmer Frannie -- #2

Farmer Frannie's fresh eggs are great!
Twenty-six ranked the best in the state.
Six more are second and two came in third
The others were fourth — that's what we heard.
Back at the farm — tucked into their house
Live even more — with a cute little mouse.
Sixteen are red, 11 are green…
And twelve of those guys are a bit in between!

Eighteen are coming — the first day of May.
To live on the farm. With Frannie to stay.
So how many hens, when all said and done
Make Frannie's farm…the best…number one?

What is the problem asking:	
List the numbers you need to solve the problem:	
What information isn't needed to solve the problem?	
Solve the problem	

Make up your own rhyming problem using at least four numbers:

From the Barn – #3

Farmer Freddie has 42 animals on his farm. He has cows, chickens and pigs. How many of each does he have? Come up with three ways the animals can be divided to equal 42.

Searching for Patterns – #4

What pattern do you see in the following string of numbers?

1. | 7 | 14 | 21 | 28 | 35 |

2. | 25 | 30 | 35 | 40 | 45 |

3. | 20 | 23 | 26 | 29 | 32 |

Use the addition table for problems 4, 5 and 6.

+	1	2	3	4	5	6
1	2	3	4	5	6	7
2	3	4	5	6	7	8
3	4	5	6	7	8	9
4	5	6	7	8	9	10
5	6	7	8	9	10	11
6	7	8	9	10	11	12

4. Look at the row for 5 in the table. Explain why the number in this row follow the pattern even, odd, even, odd.

5. Explain why the sum of two even addends is even.

6. Explain the table in complete sentences.

The Number 84 – #5

Farmer Freddy loves the number 84. How many number combination can you make. You may use all four operations, addition, subtraction, multiplication and division.

2 × 42 = 84

Farmer Fred's Fluent in Multiplication
But he needs your help... # 6

Use mental math to solve the problems for Farmer Fred.

1. Farmer Fred has a stack of hay bales. The bales are ten rows deep and three rows high.

    Problem: _____

    Mental Math Solution: _____

2. Farmer Fred has 100 chickens. Each chicken lays six eggs per week. Use mental math to tell how many eggs Farmer Fred gets in a week from his chickens.

    Problem: _____

    Mental Math Solution: _____

3. Farmer Fred married Frannie Farmer. They had 70 guests at the wedding. Half of the guests sat on the groom's side. How many sat on the bride's side?

    Problem: _____

    Mental Math Solution: _____

4. Five fabulous friends of Fred and Fannie had 100 grains of rice for the bride. How many grains of rice did the five friends have in all?

    Problem: _____

    Mental Math Solution: _____

Write your own mental math problem in the box:

Farmer Fred's New Barn – Area and Perimeter - # 7

Farmer Fred needs to build a new barn. He needs two doors and two windows. The doors should be the same size and the windows must be different sizes. Please build his barn and calculate the area and perimeter of each part and the whole below.

You must use full squares or half squares only. Be sure to color your picture.

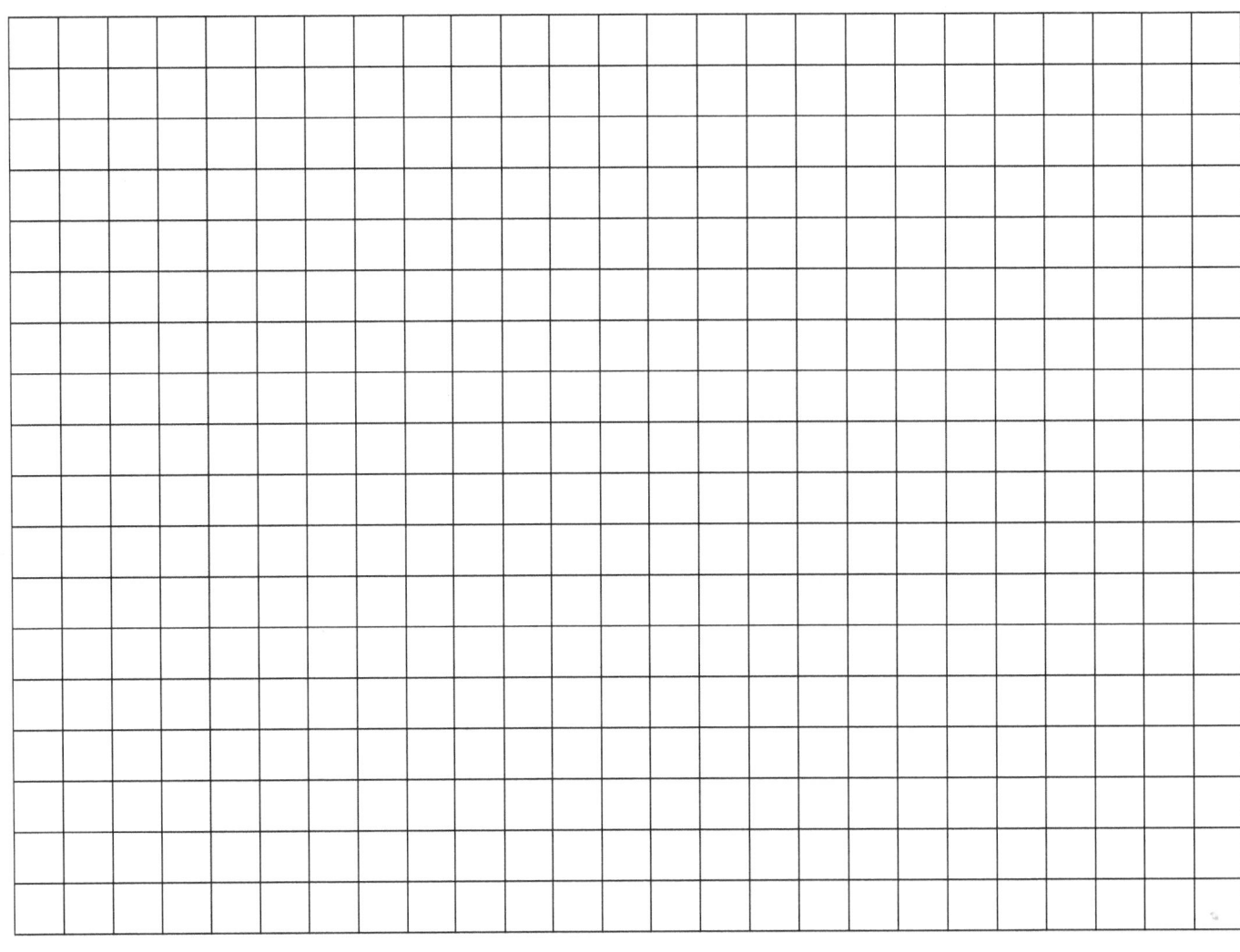

What is the area and perimeter of:

Window One: _____   Window 2: _____

Door 1:   _____   Door 2:   _____

Roof: _____   Other: (Optional) _____

Entire Barn: _____

What is the quickest way to calculate the area and perimeter of the entire barn? _____

_____

A Way With Words #8

Use the letters in the following sentence to make as many words as possible. The crazier the better!

Farmer Fred raises pigs, horses, cows and chickens.

Create a Cover for Your Favorite Book
#9

_____ by _____ is my favorite book. It is my favorite book because _____

_____

_____

_____

_____

Create a new cover for your favorite book:

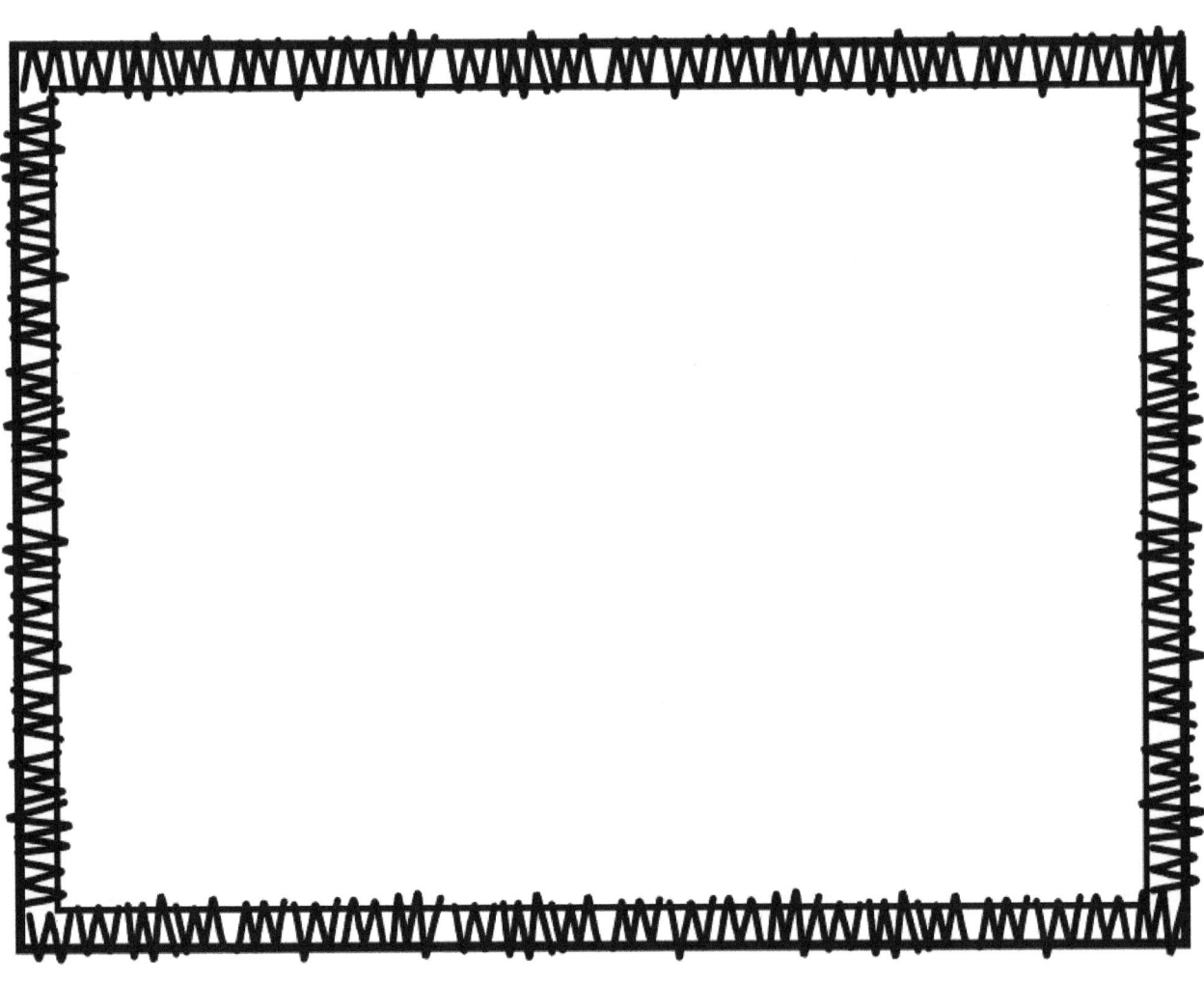

My Favorite Media in Four Panels # 10

Choose your favorite movie, television show or video clip and explain it in four pictures.

My favorite media is: _____ by: _____

Alternative Endings -- #11

A story I read this week was _____

by _____. If I could change the ending...here is how it would go...

Rain for Farmer Fred -- # 12

The weather reporter on the nightly news said that 3/10-inch of rain fell in the last 24 hours. Write the total rainfall in decimal form. _____

If 10 dimes equals 1 dollar, then 1 dime is 1/10 of a dollar.

    How many dimes are 5/10 of a dollar? _____ Write in decimal form _____

    How many dimes are 3/10 of a dollar? _____ Write in decimal form _____

    How many dimes are 10/10 of a dollar? _____ Write in decimal form _____

Frannie milks her cow, Freta, seven times per week. Each day Frannie gets 1/7 of the milk Freta gives per week. Write that in decimal form. _____.

Explain how you know you have the right answer.

_____

_____

_____

Shade in the boxes to represent 10/20.

Describe what you observe about your shading. _____

_____

_____

_____

_____

_____

_____

Finish the Fractured Fairy Tale #13

Once upon a time in a woods very close to _____ School, Jack (from the Beanstalk) decided to team up with Red to play a trick on grandma.
_____
_____
_____
_____
_____
_____
_____
_____
_____
_____
_____

Finish the Fractured Fairy Tale #14

Once upon a time, a long, long time ago, Little Red Riding Hood came across the cottage of the three bears...

_____
_____
_____
_____
_____
_____
_____
_____
_____
_____
_____
_____
_____
_____
_____
_____
_____
_____
_____
_____
_____
_____

Finish the Fractured Fairy Tale #15

Once upon a time, a long, long time ago, Little Red Riding Hood and the wolf climbed up the beanstalk... _____

What's in The Bag? #16

List all of the things Little Red Riding hood would carry in her basket. Be creative.

_____
_____
_____
_____
_____
_____
_____
_____
_____

List all of the things Jack would carry in his bag. Be creative.

_____
_____
_____
_____
_____
_____
_____

What's in The Bag? #17

Rapunzel and Prince Charming went on a vacation. What would you find in their suitcase?

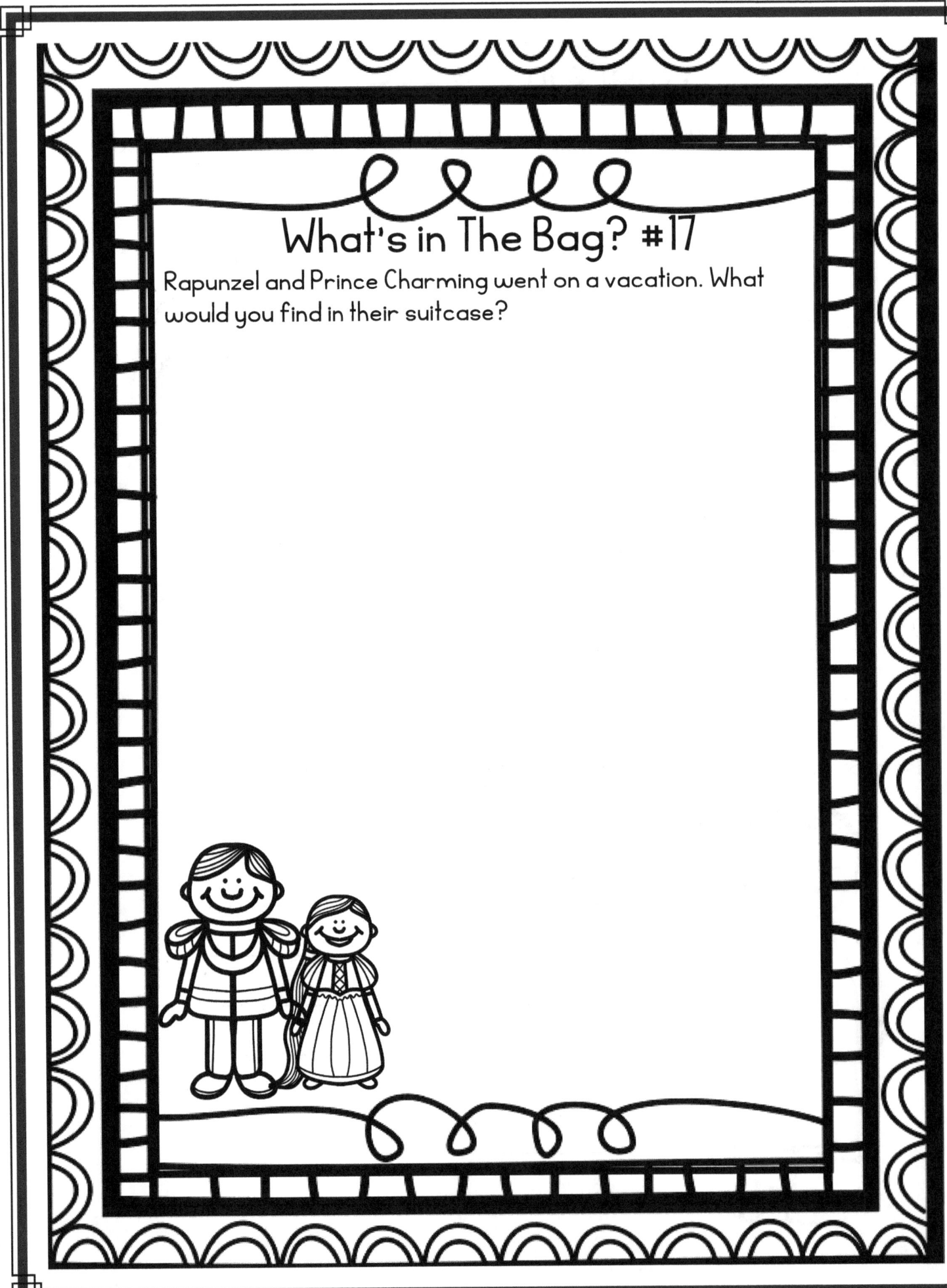

Tell Me What You Think? #18

What do you worry about most? _____
_____

What do you care about most in the entire world? _____
_____

If you could take a trip anywhere in the entire world, where would it be and why? _____
_____
_____

Describe one thing you heard in the news or saw in a newspaper or on the Internet. _____
_____
_____
_____

What are your favorite things to wear? Please use detail to describe your favorite outfit. _____
_____
_____
_____

My Hero - #19

Hero: _____

Describe your hero's physical traits: _____

_____

_____

Use detail to describe why this person is your hero: _____

_____

_____

_____

_____

All in the Word Family - 20

In each box, read the clues and add endings to the underlined word to make words that fit the word family. Remember, an ending sometimes changes the spelling of the base word.

T h i c k

More thick: _____

Most thick: _____

To become thick: _____

---

run

Run in the past: _____

Person who runs: _____

Run right now: _____

T o w e r

Two or more: _____

Very tall: _____

In the past: _____

All in the Word Family - 21

In each box, read the clues and add endings to the underlined word to make words that fit the word family. Remember, an ending sometimes changes the spelling of the base word.

P l a y

Two or more: _____

Person who plays: _____

Play in the past: _____

J u m p

Two or more: _____

Person who jumps: _____

Jump in the past: _____

F r e e z e

Turning to ice: _____

Becomes ice: _____

Where we keep ice cream: _____

Create Your Own Country #22

Country Name: _____

Describe the Climate: _____

National Animal: _____

National Flower: _____

Country Colors: _____

Most Important Laws...

Draw your country flag.

Puzzle Play – #23

Think of the word that fits in each box. Use the letters in the shaded boxes to guess the bonus word.

The season the month of April is in:

Another word for fabulous:

A month with only three letters:

United States of _____:

What does toothpaste come in?

People who go to new places:

Opposite of a lie:

Something you drink:

Rainy and windy weather:

Kings and queens may live there:

Run free
Out of school
Great big splash
Cool, cool pool.

Have some fun
No work today
Lots of time
For use to play.

What am I?

Puzzle Play – #24

Think of the word that fits in each box. Use the letters in the shaded boxes to guess the bonus word.

Loud noise in the sky:
To put together:
A man's son's son:
To help someone think:
Days of the _____ :
Color we think of for the sun:
To go on a trip:
What we breathe:
A grown-up girl:
Past tense of make:

First there was a dream,
A mouse to follow suit,
Then there was a land,
To visit is a hoot.

Hint: A dream is a wish your heart makes...

Puzzle Play – #25

Think of the word that fits in each box. Use the letters in the shaded boxes to guess the bonus word.

White fluff in the sky:

Cinderella rode in a _____:

Near in time:

A shape that is 360 degrees:

A color:

To cry out:

A crunchy fruit:

Before second:

After two:

The kind I like best is brown,
Full of gooey caramel,
It is a treat to eat...
And wonderful to smell.

It grows where it is hot
It's ground and then it's cooked
I like to eat it up!
I definitely am hooked!

Puzzle Play – #26
Fourth Grade Science – Inquiring About Rocks

Think of the word that fits in each box. Use the letters in the shaded boxes to guess the bonus word.

When I look at each rock for information:

When I write down what I see:

Look at differences and similarities:

Come to a conclusion:

More than one
Is what I see
Not to many
What can I be?

Use the words above to make up your own Puzzle and write it below:

Puzzle Play – #27

Think of the word that fits in each box. Use the letters in the shaded boxes to guess the bonus word.

The blue space on a map:

A large body of water:

Between states and continents:

These are also blue on a map:

If north is up then south is _____:

It is a big blue marble,
At least it is from space,
Orbiting 'round the sun,
It has its special place
In all the universe,
Way up in the sky
Orbiting 'round the sun
Up so very high.

In Other Words... #28

How many ways can you say the following words. In other words, how many synonyms can you come put with for each word?

like

_____
_____
_____
_____
_____
_____
_____

said

_____
_____
_____
_____
_____
_____
_____

great

_____
_____
_____
_____
_____
_____
_____

like

_____
_____
_____
_____
_____
_____
_____

In Other Words... #29

How many ways can you say the following words. In other words, how many synonyms can you come put with for each word?

went

_____
_____
_____
_____
_____
_____
_____

sad

_____
_____
_____
_____
_____
_____
_____

big

_____
_____
_____
_____
_____
_____
_____

little

_____
_____
_____
_____
_____
_____
_____

In Other Words... #30

How many ways can you say the following words. In other words, how many synonyms can you come put with for each word?

ran

_____
_____
_____
_____
_____
_____
_____

walked

_____
_____
_____
_____
_____
_____
_____

looked

_____
_____
_____
_____
_____
_____
_____

pretty

_____
_____
_____
_____
_____
_____
_____

In Other Words... #31

How many ways can you say the following words. In other words, how many synonyms can you come put with for each word?

scared
_____
_____
_____
_____
_____
_____
_____

moved
_____
_____
_____
_____
_____
_____
_____

loudly
_____
_____
_____
_____
_____
_____
_____

softly
_____
_____
_____
_____
_____
_____
_____

Your Words...My Story #32

Use the following words to write a story about anything you want.

band	pirate	ballerina	apples	Kansas
ships	trade	happy	soup	vinegar

Your Words...My Story #33

Use the following words to write a story about anything you want.

duck	ocean	bathtub	bear	box
ghost	candy	fruit	Italian	plane

Your Words...My Story #34

Use the following words to write a story about anything you want.

tree	stalk	cabin	book	wand
gold	busted	pretty	ugly	oven

Your Words...My Story #35

Use the following words to write a story about anything you want.

scrub	eat	foot	hat	goat
happy	spell	pan	rock	research

Your Words...My Story #36

Use the following words to write a story about anything you want.

cake	dirty	thief	butterfly	magnet
hanger	cap	baseball	raft	flowers

Sort it Out #37

Sort each word under the correct heading.

apple, zucchini, pear, Paris, grape, beans, New York peach, artichoke, strawberry, plum, San Francisco, Albany, celery, Toronto, carrot, cucumber, Dallas, cherry, Munich, corn, peas, Manchester, orange

Fruits: _____
_____
_____
_____

Vegetables: _____
_____
_____
_____

World Cities: _____
_____
_____
_____

Sort it Out #38

Sort each word under the correct heading.

Pants, green, shirt, red, square, yellow, circle, coat, purple, jacket, pink, blue, aqua, orange, oval, crescent, blouse, t-shirt, Triangle, violet, shoes, socks

clothes: _____

shapes: _____

colors: _____

Sort it Out #39

Sort each word under the correct heading.

Desk, chair, oak, poplar, Ohio, table, Florida, pine, Dresser, couch, walnut, cherry, Vermont, Georgia, Nightstand, end table, peach, maple, elm, Hawaii, Texas, Iowa

furniture: _____
_____
_____
_____

trees: _____
_____
_____
_____

states: _____
_____
_____
_____

Sort it Out #40

Sort each word under the correct heading.

run, dog, for, sit, cat, and, stand, tree, or, hot, house, nor, fly, boy, but, go, girl, yet, eat, desk, drink, lamp

verbs: _____

nouns: _____

conjunctions: _____

Another Word For...Synonym Word Search #41

```
A F R A I D O H A B C B A S A T
H A A S D S A O H O U G H T H K
O D B E G E G L O N E T M O L U
M K B A L T U L D S C A E N I D
Q S I C K Y K O A L A R G E N I
A N T D A H N W E I R C S D P T
G A R B E T K P K M N T G I H
A R S M E L L X Y V B C T O S O
R S R C A E S H Z N C L E N E U
B A D B F G E E P N O T E F R G
A G A D E G L A D M R I T E D H
G L D E T O W R C S M R I G H T
E C L B A N T O C H H S D G I P
D L S A M I D D L E V C L E A N
A U I Y E A N R I G A D O P Y U
C A R P E T H E R E K O H O M E
```

1. scared: _____
2. auto: _____
3. big: _____
4. bunny: _____
5. happy: _____
6. Idea: _____
7. jog: _____
8. listen: _____
9. rock: _____
10. rug: _____
11. ill: _____
12. evil: _____
13. trash: _____
14. house: _____
15. father: _____
16. neat: _____
17. center: _____
18. empty: _____
19. true: _____
20. sniff: _____

The Opposite of Antonym Word Search #42

```
S  U  B  T  R  A  C  T  A  K  D  I  T  I  X  T
A  B  E  C  K  L  M  N  E  O  L  L  B  L  M  D
F  D  L  U  I  T  S  I  N  K  G  H  E  H  J  A
E  H  O  K  R  Y  I  P  A  S  D  F  T  K  L  R
W  A  W  A  K  E  N  O  R  T  S  T  T  N  J  K
A  G  W  O  R  S  A  U  E  M  O  O  E  Z  T  T
Y  N  B  E  H  W  O  R  S  E  U  G  R  X  A  I
T  H  E  R  I  N  E  M  L  F  T  O  R  C  G  M
D  N  I  G  H  T  B  E  S  T  H  M  O  B  E  E
Y  E  L  L  O  W  M  O  R  E  R  E  P  M  B  S
D  I  R  T  Y  L  Q  R  W  E  W  T  E  N  C  N
M  E  L  O  F  U  L  L  G  D  S  U  N  O  O  T
L  A  U  G  H  A  S  G  H  J  K  G  X  E  L  O
I  F  Y  O  U  G  T  R  U  E  R  F  S  P  D  N
P  L  I  G  H  T  C  S  C  D  S  G  H  Q  S  T
W  H  Y  C  G  H  E  S  D  W  E  S  T  D  N  S
S  A  D  E  S  O  F  T  R  S  T  O  M  R  B  M
```

1. add: _____
2. above: _____
3. awake: _____
4. better: _____
5. worse: _____
6. close: _____
7. hot: _____
8. false: _____
9. day: _____
10. hungry: _____
11. happy: _____
12. hard: _____
13. dark: _____
14. east: _____
15. float: _____
16. neat: _____
17. light: _____
18. north: _____
19. less: _____
20. cry: _____

My Grocery List #43

One of your parents sends you into the grocery store and tells you to pick out what your family will eat for the next three days. Write your list below.

My Dinner #44

You have $25 to make a family meal for four people. What would you buy? Make sure you add up your total.

Steak	$8.00 per pound (you need two pounds for four people)
Hamburger	$2.80 pound (you need one pound for four people)
Potatoes	$.40 for one medium
1 whole chicken	$9.00
Lettuce	$2.50 head
Carrots	$2.00 bag
Strawberries	$3.00 basket
Pasta	$1.78 pound
Pasta Sauce	$4.56 jar
Tomatoes	$1.00 for one medium
Onions	$.50 each
Green beans	$.56 pound
Pizza	$6.79 one large frozen
Milk	$3.10 gallon
Cheese	$4.50 pound
Butter	$4.35 pound
Bread	$1.99 loaf of unsliced French
Salad Dressing	$2.30 bottle

My Menu:

Cost: (please show your work)

Trip to the Beach #45

Pretend you are an adult. You are planning a trip to the beach for one week. Plan your trip and calculate your costs.

Use the Internet to research the following costs.

Beach I am traveling to: _____

Mode of Transportation: _____

Cost of transportation: _____

Cost of renting a house or staying in a hotel:

1 day housing: _____

6 nights: _____

Cost of food: _____

_____

_____

Cost of entertainment: _____

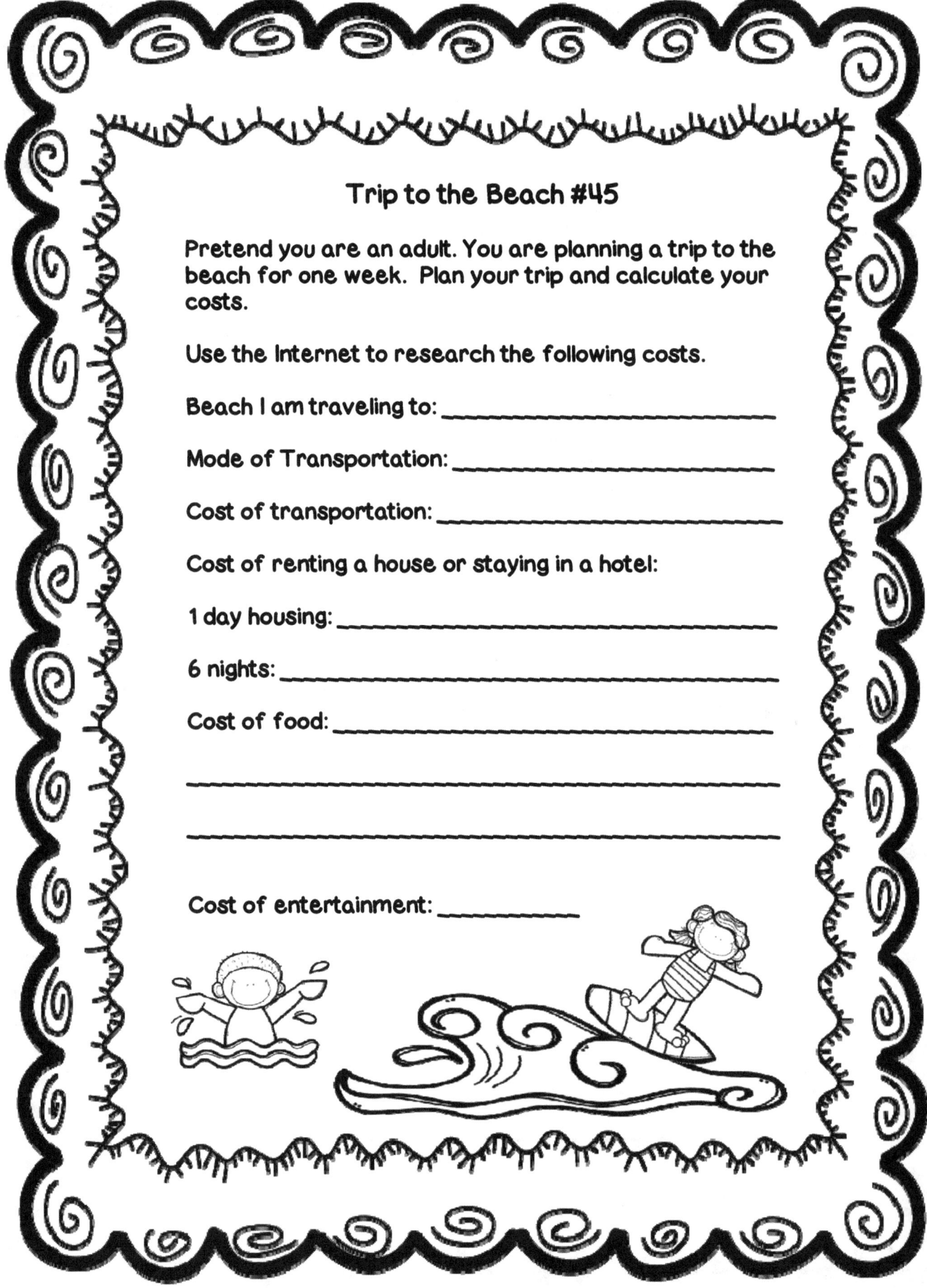

What If... #46

Image you just found out you have the winning lottery ticket. Write a paragraph describing how you would spend the money.

_____
_____
_____
_____
_____
_____
_____
_____
_____
_____

Draw one thing you would buy:

What If... #47

What if you were the principal of your school. What would you do?

_____
_____
_____
_____
_____
_____
_____
_____
_____
_____

Describe what your day would be like if you were principal.

_____
_____
_____
_____
_____
_____
_____
_____
_____
_____
_____
_____

Creative Writing from Facts... #49

Use the polar bear non-fiction facts below to write a fictional story about a polar bear named Bud who is lost.

Interesting Polar Bear Facts:
- Male polar bear can weigh up to 1500 pounds and be over 10 feet tall
- They look white, but their fur is transparent.
- Thanks to the white color, they blend with their environment.
- Polar bears have 10 cm thick layer of blubber to keep them well insulated from low temperatures and cold water.
- Their fur is dense and oily and helps keep them dry even after long time in the water.
- Although they live in cold environment (temperature can drop below minus 45 degrees of Celsius), they can easily overheat when they run (due to thick fur and blubber).
- They can run as fast as 25 miles per hour.
- They can swim 6 miles per hour. Some polar bears are seen 100 miles away from the shore.
- They can swim 70-100 miles at once.
- They spend most of their time in the water – hunting their main food source -- seal.
- They have a super sense of smell and can sense seal on the ice that is 20 miles away.
- Polar bears are omnivores (eat both plants and meat). During summer season, bears like to eat berries.
- Unlike other bears, they don't hibernate.

Creative Writing from Facts... #50

Use the hippopotamus non-fiction facts below to write a fictional story about a Hippopotamus who wants to be a pilot.

Interesting Hippopotamus Facts:
- Hippopotamuses (hippos) are third largest land mammals.
- They spend most of their life in rivers, lakes, or salty water near river mouths in Africa.
- Hippos are one of the most dangerous animals in Africa.
- Hippos can reach 12 feet in length and weigh up to 7000 pounds
- Hippos spend most of their time in water because they don't have sweat glands and that is the only way to prevent overheating.
- They can see, smell and hear when they are in the water because their eyes, nostrils and ears are positioned on the upper surface of the head.
- They have good eyesight, sense of smell and hearing.
- They create their own sunscreen. Their skin produces red oily substance that protects them from sunburn.
- They eat grass, fallen fruit, sugar cane and corn.
- Hippos can run faster than humans.
- Hippos produce loud noise that sounds like lion's roar.
- The closest relatives of hippos are whales and dolphins.

Answers

1. Fact: 14 was a dry year
   Fact: 44 acres
   Problem: 44 – 6 = 38

2. What is the problem asking? *How many chickens Farmer Frannie has*. What numbers are needed to solve the problem? *26, 6, 2, 16, 11, 12, 18*

What isn't needed? Possible answers. What prizes chickens earned. When the chickens are coming.

3. 12, 16, 14
   2, 12, 28
   5, 7, 30

4. 1. Each number is seven more than the number before 2. Each number is five more than the number before 3. Each number is one more than the number before when you add one to an even number you get and odd number and when you add one to an odd number you get an even number

If you begin with an even number and add an even number you can only get an even number.

The table increases by one both across and down. The far left row and the top row make squares. The lowest right point of each square is the answer to the addend.

5. Answers will vary
6. 1. 10 x 3 = 30; 2. 100 x 6 = 600; 3. 70 /2 = 3; 4. 5 x 100 = 500
7. Answers will vary
8. Possible words: Farmer, farm, Fred, raise, pork, chick, marker, cow, mark, park, charmer, charm...
9. Answer will vary – book cover.
10. Answer will vary – favorite media.
11. Answers will vary.
12. 0.3;
How many dimes are 5/10 of a dollar?   5 Write in decimal form 0.5
How many dimes are 3/10 of a dollar?   3 Write in decimal form 0.3
How many dimes are 10/10 of a dollar? 10 Write in decimal form 1

#20	thicker	ran	towers
	thickest	runner	towering
	thicken	running	towered
#21	plays	jumps	freezing
	Player	jumper	frozen
	Played	jumped	freezer

#22 Answers will vary

#23 summertime

The season the month of April is in: s p r i n g
Another word for fabulous: s u p e r
A month with only three letters: m a y
United States of _____: A m e r i c a
What does toothpaste come in?   t u b e
People who go to new places: e x p l o r e r s
Opposite of a lie: t r u t h

Something you drink:	j	u	i	c	e	
Rainy and windy weather:	s	t	o	r	m	y
Kings and queens may live there:	c	a	s	t	l	e

#24 Disneyland

Loud noise in the sky:	t	h	u	n	d	e	r
To put together:	j	o	i	n			
A man's son's son:	g	r	a	n	d	s	o	n
To help someone think:	r	e	m	i	n	d
Days of the _____ :	w	e	e	k
Color we think of for the sun:	y	e	l	l	o	w
To go on a trip:	t	r	a	v	e	l
What we breathe:	a	i	r
A grown-up girl:	w	o	m	a	n
Past tense of make:	m	a	d	e

#25 chocolate

White fluff in the sky:	c	l	o	u	d
Cinderella rode in a _____:	c	o	a	c	h
Near in time:	s	o	o	o
A shape that is 360 degrees:	c	i	r	c	l	w
A color:	o	r	a	n	g	e
To cry out:	c	a	l	l
A crunchy fruit:	a	p	p	l	e
Before second:	f	i	r	s	t
After two:	t	h	r	e	e

26 some

When I look at each rock for information:	o	b	s	e	r	v	e
When I write down what I see:	r	e	c	o	r	d
Look at differences and similarities:	c	o	m	p	a	r	e
Come to a conclusion:	i	n	f	e	r

27 world

The blue space on a map:	w	a	t	e	r
A large body of water:	o	c	e	a	n
Between states and continents:	c	o	u	n	t	r	y
These are also blue on a map:	l	a	k	e	s
If north is up then south is _____:	d	o	w	n

28 - # 36 Answers will vary

37 Fruits: apple, pear, grape, peach, strawberry, plum, cherry, orange; vegetables: zucchini, beans, artichoke, celery, carrot, cucumber, corn, peas; world cities: Paris, New York, San Francisco, Albany, Toronto, Dallas, Munich, Manchester

38 clothes: pants, shirt, coat, jacket, blouse, t-shirt, shoes, socks; shapes: square, circle, oval, crescent, triangle; colors: green, red, yellow, purple, pink, blue, aqua, orange, violet

#39: furniture: desk, chair, table, couch, dresser, bed, nightstand, end table; trees: oak, poplar, pine, walnut, cherry, peach, maple, elm; states: Ohio, Florida, Maine, Vermont, Georgia, Hawaii, Texas, Iowa

#40: verbs: run, sit, stand, hop, fly, go, eat, drink; nouns: dog, cat, tree, house, boy, girl, desk, lamp; conjunctions: for, and, or, nor, but, yet

#41.

A	F	R	A	I	D	O	H	A	B	C	B	A	S	A	T
H	A	A	S	D	S	A	O	H	O	U	G	H	T	H	K
O	D	B	E	G	E	G	L	O	N	E	T	M	O	L	U
M	K	B	A	L	T	U	L	D	S	C	A	E	N	I	D
Q	S	I	C	K	Y	K	O	A	L	A	R	G	E	N	I
A	N	T	D	A	H	N	W	E	I	R	C	S	D	P	T
G	A	R	B	E	T	K	P	K	M	N	T	G	T	I	H
A	R	S	M	E	L	L	X	Y	V	B	C	T	O	S	O
R	S	R	C	A	E	S	H	Z	N	C	L	E	N	E	U
B	A	D	B	F	G	E	E	P	N	O	T	E	F	R	G
A	G	A	D	E	G	L	A	D	M	R	I	T	E	D	H
G	L	D	E	T	O	W	R	C	S	M	R	I	G	H	T
E	C	L	B	A	N	T	O	C	H	H	S	D	G	I	P
D	L	S	A	M	I	D	D	L	E	V	C	L	E	A	N
A	U	I	Y	E	A	N	R	I	G	A	D	O	P	Y	U
C	A	R	P	E	T	H	E	R	E	K	O	H	O	M	E

#42

S	U	B	T	R	A	C	T	A	K	D	I	T	I	X	T
A	B	E	C	K	L	M	N	E	O	L	L	B	L	M	D
F	D	L	U	I	T	S	I	N	K	G	H	E	H	J	A
E	H	O	K	R	Y	I	P	A	S	D	F	T	K	L	R
W	A	W	A	K	E	N	O	R	T	S	T	T	N	J	K
A	G	W	O	R	S	A	U	E	M	O	O	E	Z	T	T
Y	N	B	E	H	W	O	R	S	E	U	G	R	X	A	I
T	H	E	R	I	N	E	M	L	F	T	O		C	G	M
D	N	I	G	H	T	B	E	S	T	H	M	O	B	E	E
Y	E	L	L	O	W	M	O	R	E	R	E	P	M	B	S
D	I	R	T	Y	L	Q	R	W	E	W	T	E	N	C	N
M	E	L	O	F	U	L	L	G	D	S	U	N	O	O	T
L	A	U	G	H	A	S	G	H	J	K	G	X	E	L	O
I	F	Y	O	U	G	T	R	U	E		F	S	P	D	N
P	L	I	G	H	T	C	S	C	D	S	G	H	Q	S	T
W	H	Y	C	G	H	E	S	D	W	E	S	T	D	N	S
S	A	D	E	S	O	F	T	R	S	T	O	M	R	B	M

#43-#50 Answers will vary

Credits

Farm Clips:

All Other Clip Art and All Borders
Krista Wallden:

My Pinterest: https://www.pinterest.com/epinotti/

Check Out Some of My Other Products at the Links Below

www.ingramcontent.com/pod-product-compliance
Lightning Source LLC
Chambersburg PA
CBHW081022040426
42444CB00014B/3316